Mr Steggels
Selective Achievement Tests
Level 1

Suitable for ages 7 – 9

Each test contains 35 mixed questions

- 15 general ability
- 10 reading comprehension
- 10 mathematics

A score summary chart is printed at the end of each test

Contents

Test 1	page 2
Test 2	page 12
Test 3	page 22
Test 4	page 32
Test 5	page 42

Solutions

Test 1	page 52
Test 2	page 53
Test 3	page 55
Test 4	page 57
Test 5	page 59

Copyright © 2017 Simon Steggels
All rights reserved

No part of this book may be reproduced, stored in a retrieval system, communicated or transmitted in any form or by any means without prior written permission. All inquiries should be made to the publisher.

ISBN 978-0-6480967-0-2

Published by
Advanced Instruction Pty Ltd
www.advancedinstruction.com.au

© MR STEGGELS ADVANCED INSTRUCTION PTY LTD

Test 1

Read the text and answer questions 1—5

Age	What can a child do?
Birth to 3 months	Hold up head for a few seconds Suck Hold and pull Make a fist
3 months to 6 months	Roll over Pull body forward Reach and grab Bring object to mouth Shake and play with objects
6 to 9 months	Crawl Grab and pull objects Move object from one hand to the other
9 to 12 months	Sit up Stand Walk Pick up and throw objects Roll a ball Hold objects between thumb and finger
1 to 2 years	Pick up things while standing Walk backwards Walk up and down stairs Move to music Scribble Turn knobs and handles
2 to 3 years	Run Jump Kick a ball Turn pages of a book Draw a circle Hold a crayon

© MR STEGGELS ADVANCED INSTRUCTION PTY LTD

1. This text is mainly about

    A growing and changing
    B how to take care of a small child
    C playing
    D what kids need to grow

2. The main purpose of this text is to

    A give information
    B sell something
    C explain what makes kids grow
    D retell an event

3. Which is true?

    A A one year old child can run
    B A child can crawl at 3 months
    C A baby can make a fist
    D A two year old child cannot walk backwards

4. At what age can a child first open a door with a handle?

    A 3 months to 6 months
    B 1 year to 2 years
    C 2 years to 3 years
    D birth to 3 months

5. By 12 months, a child should be able to

    A turn the pages of a book
    B scribble
    C walk up and down stairs
    D pick up and throw a ball

6. Which letters are missing in this series?

| G | I | K | ? | O |

   A   P
   B   L
   C   N
   D   M

7. A swimming pool is 11m long and 6m wide. What is the distance around the edge of the pool?

   A   12m
   B   17m
   C   22m
   D   34m

8. In a certain code, the words **and** and **got** are written **5V%** and **K7&** in that order. How would **dong** be written using this code?

   A   %75K
   B   K5V&
   C   &V75
   D   %7VK

9. At 9am the temperature was 12°C. By 11am, it had gone up by 7°C. By 2pm, it had gone down by 3°C. The temperature at 2pm was

   A   22°C
   B   21°C
   C   16°C
   D   8°C

10. The word most opposite in meaning to **rude** is

    A   unrude
    B   happy
    C   okay
    D   polite

© MR STEGGELS ADVANCED INSTRUCTION PTY LTD

11. Which is the odd one out?

12. Which word does not belong in this group of similar words?

   A   stamp
   B   swamp
   C   damp
   D   clamp

13. I am thinking of two numbers. They add to 12. The difference between them is 8. One of the numbers must be:

   A   2
   B   4
   C   6
   D   8

14. What two operations must be added to the following number sentence to make it correct?

$$2 \; ? \; 6 \; ? \; 5 \; = \; 7$$

   A   add then divide
   B   multiply then add
   C   add then subtract
   D   multiply then subtract

15. Which word can be placed before these four words to make new, compound words?

   _____line   _____side   _____run   _____fit

   A   side
   B   in
   C   out
   D   under

Read the text and answer questions 16—20

Best friends

Sarah and I are like two peas in a pod—or so our mothers say.

We always stick together. We have the same hair colour. We go to the same school. We are in the same grade, but different classes. We sit next to each other at recess and lunch.

We play netball in the same team—the Blue Jays. We watch the same television shows and listen to the same music. We even share the same favourite colour—yellow. We both like pizza and our favourite ice cream is strawberry.

Sarah is two months older than me. My birthday is in July. Last year we helped to **organise** each other's birthday parties. Next year, we want to have a double party for both of our birthdays. We will invite everyone from school. We want to go to Wet World Water Park. It will be such fun with a big group.

Sarah and I first met when her family moved into the house across the street. That was three years ago. Our mothers became friends right away, so we started playing together. We went to preschool together.

It's great having a best friend. I don't know what I would do without Sarah. I wouldn't have anyone to play with at school. I wouldn't have anyone to plan birthdays with. I wouldn't have anyone to talk to.

Life is much more fun with a best friend.

© MR STEGGELS ADVANCED INSTRUCTION PTY LTD

16. The saying **like two peas in a pod** means that the best friends

    A   are happy
    B   are so similar you can't tell them apart
    C   have the same colour hair
    D   like eating peas

17. Which is a fact, not an opinion?

    A   It's great having a best friend
    B   Sarah and I are like two peas in a pod
    C   We watch the same television shows and listen to the same music
    D   Life is much more fun with a best friend

18. The word **organise** can best be replaced with

    A   celebrate
    B   sort
    C   shape
    D   arrange

19. In what month is Sarah's birthday?

    A   July
    B   September
    C   June
    D   May

20. The author and Sarah started playing together because

    A   their mothers became friends right away
    B   they are in the same class
    C   life is much more fun with a best friend
    D   they went to the same preschool

© MR STEGGELS ADVANCED INSTRUCTION PTY LTD

21. Someone who **sells fruit and vegetables** is called a

    A vegetarian
    B greengrocer
    C landlord
    D green keeper

22. Find the rule connecting the numbers in the first row with those in the second row. Which number completes the pattern?

9	10	8	5
12	14	10	?

    A 2
    B 4
    C 6
    D 9

23. I tossed a six-sided die. What is the chance that I roll an even number?

    A 1 out of 6
    B 2 out of 6
    C 1 out of 2
    D none of the above

24. Which is the odd one out?

    A parsley
    B mint
    C clam
    D basil

25. How many squares of any size are in this shape?

    A 6
    B 7
    C 8
    D 9

© MR STEGGELS ADVANCED INSTRUCTION PTY LTD

26. **Easy** is to **difficult** as **fresh** is to

   A   rotten
   B   healthy
   C   dirty
   D   unfresh

27. Here are results from a high jump competition. Who improved the most from their first jump to their second jump?

Results	John	Sarah	Ali	Chivani
First jump	1.85m	1.56m	2.02m	2.10m
Second jump	2.01m	1.66m	2.13m	2.25m

   A   John
   B   Sarah
   C   Ali
   D   Chivani

28. Rearrange these words into a coherent sentence

   still   teacher   students   his   to   the   sit   told

   If the first word in the sentence is **The**, the last word of the sentence is

   A   students
   B   teacher
   C   told
   D   still

29. In a certain code, **he** is written 39 and **at** is written 85. How would **teeth** be written using this code?

   A   53353
   B   59933
   C   59953
   D   95583

30. People were asked about their favourite sport. This sector graph shows their answers. Nine people chose netball. How many people altogether were asked about their favourite sport?

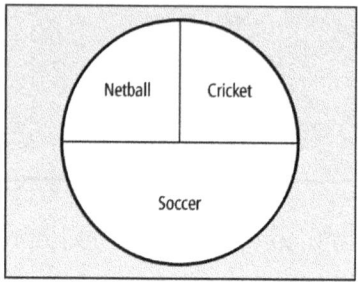

    A   9
    B   18
    C   36
    D   54

31. Unscramble these words to find the one that is **not a body part**

    A   btmuh
    B   otof
    C   klwa
    D   thera

32. Which shape is next in the pattern?

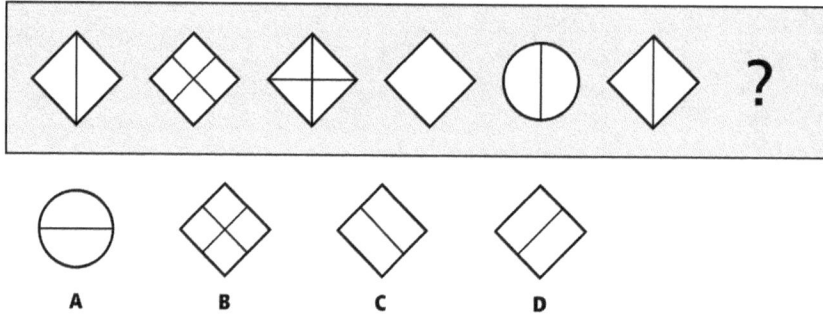

33. I gave half of my money to a friend. I then spent $2. I had $3 left over. How much money did I have to begin with?

    A $8
    B $10
    C $12
    D   none of the above

34. Solve this visual puzzle

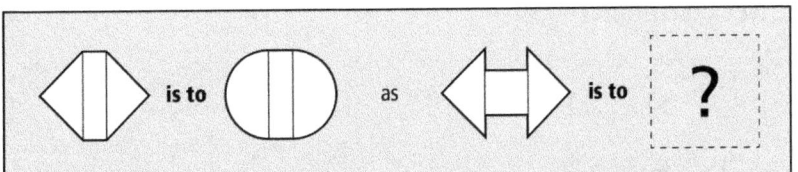

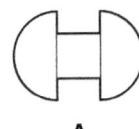 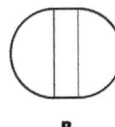 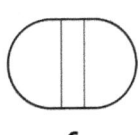 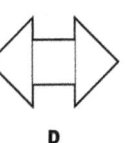
A　　　　　B　　　　　C　　　　　D

35. In a certain code, the letter A = 2, B = 4, C = 6 and so on. In the same code, L =

    A   20
    B   22
    C   24
    D   26

© MR STEGGELS ADVANCED INSTRUCTION PTY LTD

END OF TEST

Test 2

Read the text and answer questions 1—5

Out of time

Thomas had to be back in time for dinner. His mother thought he was playing in his bedroom. But Thomas was not in his bedroom. He wasn't even in his house. Thomas wasn't in the right place—or time.

One week earlier, Thomas had found the strange looking watch. It was in a drawer in an old desk. The desk had belonged to his grandfather. It was in a spare room. At first, Thomas thought the watch was a piece of junk. But when it started to hum and glow, he was excited, so he put it on.

Thomas saw that the hands on the watch weren't moving. So he **wound** the watch by turning the knob on the side. Suddenly, the hands starting spinning. They were moving so quickly Thomas thought that the watch would break apart. Then everything changed.

The room around him was gone. The house was gone. Thomas found himself standing in a huge city. Buildings as high as the clouds shot up around him. They were covered in lights and writing that Thomas had never seen before. Flying cars zoomed over his head. People floated past on tiny boards. They were talking into their silver helmets.

The watch got warm. The hands started to spin again. The people were gone. The city around him was gone.

Thomas found himself in a forest. The trees were so thick with leaves that they blocked out the sun. Strange sounds filled his ears. Animal sounds—but not any animals that Thomas had heard before. Suddenly, out of the bushes, a huge head appeared. It was as big as a truck! The eyes were as big as dinner plates. Then Thomas saw the teeth—rows of huge, sharp teeth. The monster let out a roar that knocked Thomas off his feet! Then it ran toward him. The ground shook!

Thomas looked at his watch. The glass was cracked...

© MR STEGGELS ADVANCED INSTRUCTION PTY LTD

1. Why had Thomas never heard such animal sounds before?

    A   He had never been in a forest
    B   Strange sounds filled his ears
    C   The animals are from another time
    D   It doesn't say in the text

2. What happens second?

    A   Thomas thought the watch was a piece of junk
    B   The watch got warm
    C   The watch started to glow and hum
    D   A huge head appeared from the bushes

3. The word **wound** as it is used in the text sounds like

    A   spooned
    B   ground
    C   wand
    D   none of the above

4. What caused Thomas to be taken to another place?

    A   The watch started to hum and glow
    B   The hands started spinning
    C   Thomas wound the watch by turning the knob on the side
    D   Thomas put on the watch

5. We can conclude that the first place Thomas went to was

    A   in the past
    B   in the future
    C   a city near his house
    D   none of the above

© MR STEGGELS ADVANCED INSTRUCTION PTY LTD

6. The saying **to turn your back on someone** means that you

    A   say nasty things about them
    B   get angry with them
    C   welcome them
    D   ignore them

7. **Finish** is to **end** as **crooked** is to

    A   bent
    B   teeth
    C   crook
    D   straight

8. Complete the following saying

    As stubborn as a _____ .

    A   horse
    B   donkey
    C   mule
    D   cat

9. I am thinking of 2 numbers. They add together to make 12. One number is double the other. The difference between these two numbers is

    A   2
    B   4
    C   8
    D   10

10. How many more squares are needed to make this pattern a square?

    A   5
    B   8
    C   10
    D   25

Use this timetable to answer questions 11—12

Time	Activity	Time	Activity
9.00am – 9.40am	reading groups	11.30am – 12.10pm	math problems
9.40am – 10.20am	spelling	12.10pm – 1.00pm	math games
10.20am – 11.00am	writing	1.00pm – 2.00pm	lunch
11.00am – 11.20am	recess	2.00pm – 3.00pm	science / art

11. How many minutes are spent on math activities?

    A   30 minutes
    B   40 minutes
    C   60 minutes
    D   90 minutes

12. Which is false?

    A   Lunch is twice as long as recess
    B   Most classes are 40 minutes long
    C   There are two hours of lessons before recess
    D   The spelling lesson follows reading groups

---

13. Rearrange all of the words to make a coherent sentence.

    get   the   doctor   rest   some   to   said

    If the first word is **The**, the last word of the new sentence is

    A   doctor
    B   said
    C   some
    D   rest

---

14. I bought some sugar cubes. They were 1cm wide. They came in a box. The box was also a cube. It was 3cm wide. How many sugar cubes were in the box altogether?

    A   9
    B   12
    C   27
    D   36

© MR STEGGELS ADVANCED INSTRUCTION PTY LTD

15. Which word means **got onto an aeroplane**?

    A   stepped on
    B   took off
    C   runway
    D   boarded

16. What number is missing from this number sentence?

    $$4 \times \underline{} = 8 \times 3$$

    A   4
    B   6
    C   8
    D   24

17. **Milk** is to **carton** as **flowers** is to

    A   vase
    B   garden
    C   bunch
    D   birthday

18. If the shaded section of this shape is worth 1, what is the whole shape worth?

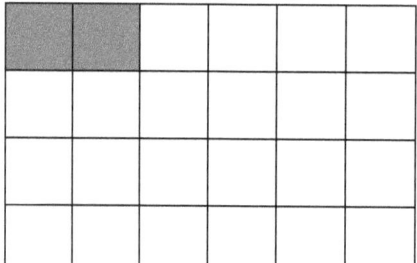

    A   24
    B   18
    C   12
    D   6

19. I started at school and rode to the shop. Along the way, I saw this sign. How far did I ride?

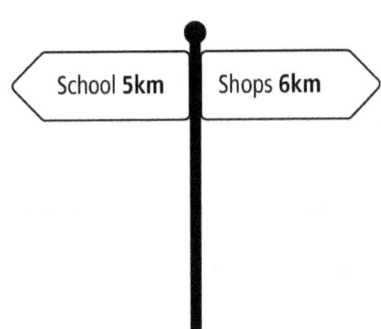

- A   5 km
- B   6 km
- C   1 km
- D   11 km

20. Which shape is a reflection of the shape on the left?

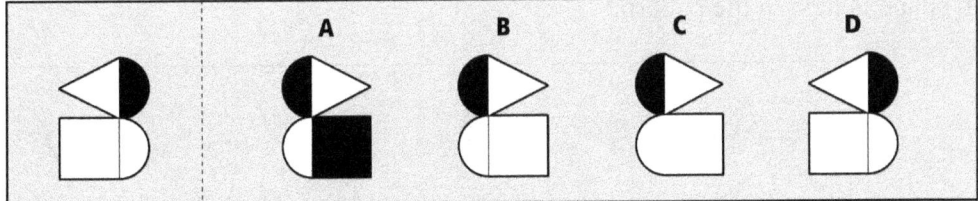

21. If **wide** + **hear** = **dear** then **deli** + **soft** =

- A   deft
- B   lift
- C   silo
- D   eoft

22. Which word can be used to end the first word and begin the second?

pick_____ / _____load

- A   truck
- B   fruit
- C   up
- D   un

© MR STEGGELS ADVANCED INSTRUCTION PTY LTD

23. The letters in **alert** can be rearranged to make a new word meaning

    A   a story
    B   aware of danger
    C   cousin
    D   at a time in the future

24. Sam had 36 bunches of flowers to deliver. At the first stop, he delivered 1 bunch. At the second stop, he delivered 2 bunches. At the third stop, he delivered 3 bunches and so on. How many stops did Sam make to deliver all 36 bunches of flowers?

    A   8
    B   7
    C   6
    D   5

25. Which shape is next in the pattern?

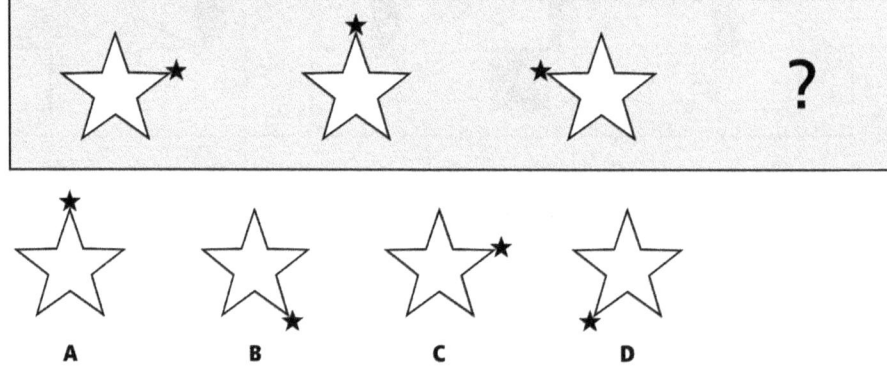

26. Which word has the same meaning as **grow**?

    A   seed
    B   increase
    C   big
    D   decrease

© MR STEGGELS ADVANCED INSTRUCTION PTY LTD

27. Which word belongs in this group of similar words?

clear   cloudy   rainbow   lightning

- A   thunderstorm
- B   umbrella
- C   sun
- D   season

28. Which word can be made from the same letters as **stare**?

- A   rates
- B   taser
- C   tears
- D   all of the above

29. I am more than 40 but less than 52. I am an even number. How many different numbers could I be?

- A   11
- B   7
- C   6
- D   5

30. A **kitchen** always has

- A   chairs
- B   a table
- C   an oven
- D   a microwave

© MR STEGGELS ADVANCED INSTRUCTION PTY LTD

Read the text and answer questions 31—35

Easter hat

Make a simple hat for your school Easter hat parade!

You will need:

    soft tape measure
    bright coloured cardboard—big enough to fit around your head
    Easter stencils—see below
    coloured feathers
    glitter glue stick
    crayons
    glue or a stapler
    safety scissors

Method:

1. Use soft tape measure to measure around your head.
2. Add 10cm to length for overlap.
3. Cut strip of cardboard 15cm wide and length you just measured.
4. Glue or staple cardboard strip into circle with overlap.
5. Colour Easter stencils with crayons.
6. Carefully cut out stencils and glue onto cardboard.
7. Glue feathers onto hat.
8. Decorate hat with glitter glue stick.
9. Wait for glue to dry.
10. Try on your Easter hat.

Have a great time at your Easter hat parade in your colourful hat!

© MR STEGGELS ADVANCED INSTRUCTION PTY LTD

31. This text is meant for

   A   adults who want to make an Easter hat for their child
   B   kids who want to make their own Easter hat
   C   teachers who want to make Easter hats with a class of 30 children
   D   teenagers only

32. Which is true?

   A   The length of the overlap is 15 cm
   B   The stencils are not included with the text
   C   You can use glue or a stapler to fix the cardboard into a circle
   D   Black cardboard is best for this Easter hat

33. What should you do second?

   A   Carefully cut out the stencils
   B   Decorate the hat with glitter glue
   C   Colour in Easter stencils with crayons
   D   Cut a strip of cardboard

34. Which two steps could be swapped?

   A   steps 2 and 3
   B   steps 7 and 9
   C   steps 7 and 8
   D   steps 5 and 6

35. Which is the only step that does not begin with a command verb?

   A   step 1
   B   step 6
   C   step 9
   D   step 10

© MR STEGGELS ADVANCED INSTRUCTION PTY LTD

END OF TEST

Test 3

1. I have three playing cards—King, Queen & Jack. The Queen is to the left of the Jack. The King is to the right of the Queen. The Jack is to the left of the King. What is the order of the cards from left to right?

   A   King, Queen, Jack
   B   Queen, King, Jack
   C   King, Jack, Queen
   D   Queen, Jack, King

2. **Crowd** is to **people** as _____ is to _____.

   A   aunt   uncle
   B   rabbit   burrow
   C   flock   sheep
   D   fish   sea

3. I am thinking of two words that sound the same but are spelt differently. Their meanings are

   (1) attached with string
   (2) the rising and falling of the sea

   Both of these words begin with the letter

   A   p
   B   t
   C   s
   D   b

4. In a certain code, **posh** is written % # @ !

   How would the word **hops** be written in the same code?

   A   # ! % @
   B   ! # % @
   C   ! # @ %
   D   ! @ % #

© MR STEGGELS ADVANCED INSTRUCTION PTY LTD

5. I went to the shop with a $5 note. I spent $1.65 on a pencil. How much change should I get?

   A $4.45
   B $4.35
   C $3.45
   D $3.35

6. The word most similar to **smooth** is

   A   even
   B   rough
   C   soothe
   D   plain

7. Which shape has six faces that are squares?

   A   square pyramid
   B   rectangular prism
   C   triangular prism
   D   cube

8. What number is missing from this pattern?

   1, 2, 4, 7, 11, 16, ___

   A   20
   B   22
   C   24
   D   26

9. A **house** always has

   A   a family
   B   a garage
   C   walls
   D   a fence

© MR STEGGELS ADVANCED INSTRUCTION PTY LTD

Read the text and answer questions 10—14

Staying safe around water

Playing in the water is lots of fun. But it can also be _____ (10). People like to relax in pools, lakes, rivers and at beaches. But not everyone can swim.

How can you keep yourself and others safe around water?

- Make sure that everyone knows how to _____ (11). If not, they need lessons before going into the water. They should wear a life jacket until they are able to swim.
- Check how deep the water is before you jump in. If the water isn't deep enough, you can hurt yourself very badly.
- Check the water for spiders, logs, glass and rocks. Some rocks have shells on them that are very _____ (12).
- Never swim near a boat ramp or near water skiers or jet skis. They can't see you in the water.
- Always swim _____ (13) the yellow flags at the beach. Listen to the lifesavers. Swim where they can see you.
- Don't swim when waves are big or the water is moving quickly. You could get dragged out to sea.
- Read warning signs that tell you if it is safe to swim or not.
- Never swim alone.
- Check how cold the water is before jumping in. Very cold water can make it hard for you to _____ (14).

These are important things to remember when you are around water. So, have fun in the water but please stay safe.

© MR STEGGELS ADVANCED INSTRUCTION PTY LTD

10. Choose the most suitable word for position 10

    A   enjoyable
    B   healthy
    C   dangerous
    D   safe

11. Choose the most suitable word(s) for position 11

    A   have fun
    B   dive
    C   splash
    D   swim

12. Choose the most suitable word for position 12

    A   sharp
    B   pretty
    C   white
    D   valuable

13. Choose the most suitable word(s) for position 13

    A   to
    B   outside
    C   between
    D   away from

14. Choose the most suitable word for position 14

    A   see
    B   do freestyle
    C   float
    D   breathe

© MR STEGGELS ADVANCED INSTRUCTION PTY LTD

15. How many of the shape A are needed to cover shape B?

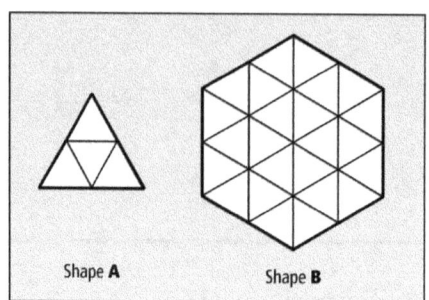

A   3
B   6
C   9
D   12

16. Which solid has the smallest number of corners?

A   triangular prism
B   rectangular prism
C   square pyramid
D   cube

17. Which shape completes the second pair in the same way as the first?

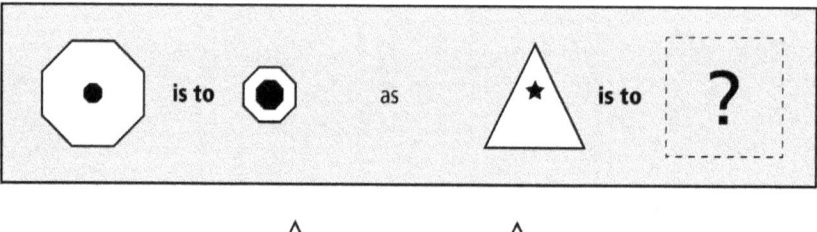

A   B   C   D

18. What should you do with a **trifle**?

A   shoot it
B   wear it
C   play it
D   eat it

19. Choose two words, one from each group, to make a new word.

Group A	walk	over	light	hand
Group B	water	day	shake	well

The new word beings with

A   w
B   s
C   l
D   h

20. In a certain code, the words **he**, **so** and **oh** are written 67, 74 and 45 but not necessarily in that order. How would the word **shoe** be written in the same code?

A   6457
B   6745
C   6475
D   6547

21. Which letter will end the first word and start the second word?

das ___ / ___ int

A   e
B   m
C   k
D   h

22. What fraction of the shape is shaded?

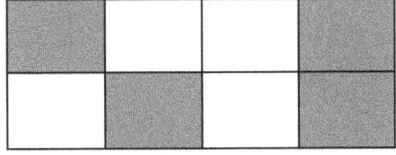

A   ⅜
B   ⅔
C   ½
D   ⅖

23. School starts at the time shown on the clock. Recess is at 10:00 am. How many minutes from the start of school until recess?

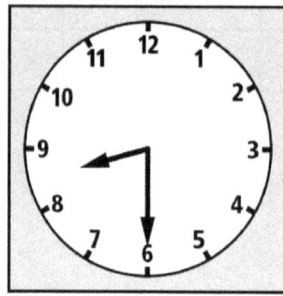

- A 30 minutes
- B 60 minutes
- C 90 minutes
- D none of the above

24. In a certain code, the word **rim** is written **qhl**. In the same code, how would **wax** be written?

- A vzw
- B vzy
- C vbw
- D vby

25. Rearrange the letters in each word and choose which one is **a musical instrument**

- A acre
- B abet
- C tabu
- D anew

26. The saying **at the drop of a hat** means

- A be careful to not drop your hat
- B willing to do something right away
- C time to start over
- D things fall very quickly when you drop them

27. Which colour will the spinner land on more than any other?

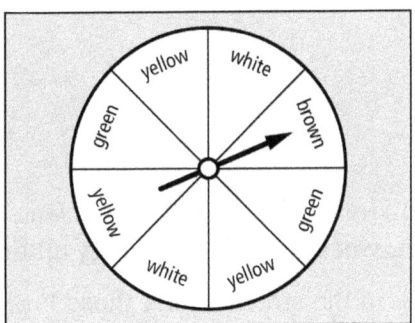

   A   white
   B   green
   C   yellow
   D   brown

28. One day ago it was Friday. What day of the week will it be one week from today?

   A   Friday
   B   Saturday
   C   Sunday
   D   Thursday

29. Which is the odd one out?

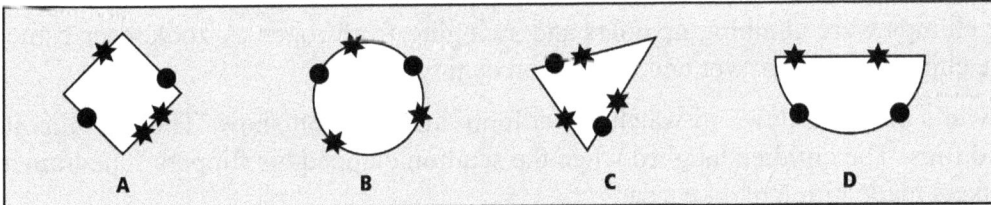

30. Choose the most suitable words to complete the sentence

   I (played / ran / swam) across the (sand / classroom / lake) to the (pool / teacher / island).

   A   played   classroom   teacher
   B   ran   sand   island
   C   swam   lake   island
   D   played   sand   pool

© MR STEGGELS ADVANCED INSTRUCTION PTY LTD

Read the text and answer questions 31—35

Zoo visit

Howie hurried to his classroom. His teacher, Ms Stewart, was waiting at her desk. Howie sat patiently while the other kids turned up. Then, when the bell went, they all lined up outside.

Howie could see the bus waiting in the street. It had those big, high comfy seats. The zoo was an hour away, so it would be a nice trip.

The bus went through the city. People walked quickly along the streets. They were dressed for work. The bus went over The Harbour Bridge. Howie saw a huge, white ship. It was right next to the bridge. There was a climbing wall and even a water slide on the top. It looked like such fun!

Finally, the bus pulled up outside the zoo. Howie was first off the bus. His teacher told him to wait at the entrance. His classmates lined up behind him.

A man came out to meet them. He and Ms Stewart shook hands. He told Howie's class that his name was James and he was going to take them around the zoo to show them all of the animals.

The first place they went was the Aussie bush area. Howie saw kangaroos and emus. Koalas were sleeping up high in the gum trees. James told the children to look for two echidnas in a special area, but Howie could only find one.

The next place they visited was the African safari. Howie saw giraffes being fed. He saw elephants and zebras. The lions were in a separate area behind glass. They looked very lazy. Howie saw their huge, sharp teeth when they yawned.

Next, James took Howie's class to see the chimpanzees. There were babies holding onto their mothers. Some of the chimps were climbing up poles and swinging from ropes. A zookeeper came with a basket of bananas. The chimpanzees ran over and started screeching at her.

Then Howie's class sat down to watch the dolphin and sea lion show. The dolphins jumped out of the water and did flips. The children laughed when the sea lion clapped his flippers. The trainer gave him a fish. His big whiskers made him look like a cat.

After lunch, James took Howie's class to see the Tasmanian devils. They were in a special area. James said it was because there are not many of them left in the wild. The zoo was taking extra care to make sure they kept having babies.

On the way back to school in the bus, Howie fell asleep. He dreamed about the animals he had seen at the zoo. It was a day he would never forget.

© MR STEGGELS ADVANCED INSTRUCTION PTY LTD

31. This text can best be described as

    A   a narrative that tells an imaginative story
    B   a recount about a day at the zoo
    C   an argument about why zoos are special places
    D   an information report on zoo animals

32. Just before lunch, James took the class to see the

    A   chimpanzees
    B   dolphin and sea lion show
    C   Tasmanian devils
    D   African safari

33. What happened third?

    A   A zookeeper came with a basket of bananas
    B   Howie saw the giraffes being fed
    C   The sea lion clapped his flippers
    D   Howie's teacher told him to wait at the entrance

34. What is the most likely reason that the lions were in a separate area behind glass?

    A   They are very lazy and need to sleep a lot
    B   Lions are not found in Africa
    C   They don't like loud noises especially noisy school children
    D   They are predators and might attack the other animals

35. Which is true?

    A   The sea lion jumped out of the water and did flips
    B   The chimpanzees screeched because they were angry
    C   Howie was the first to arrive at his classroom
    D   There was only one echidna in the special area

© MR STEGGELS ADVANCED INSTRUCTION PTY LTD

END OF TEST

Test 4

1. The letters in the word **meats** can be rearranged to make a word meaning

    A   sports
    B   a white mist of water
    C   eat
    D   wild

2. Rearrange the words below to make the best sentence

                     is   popular   birthday   pizza   at   party   a   very

    If the third word is **very**, what is the last word?

    A   pizza
    B   party
    C   birthday
    D   popular

3. If I kept adding numbers to this grid, in which column would I write the number 24?

P	Q	R	S
1	2	3	4
8	7	6	5

    A   column P
    B   column Q
    C   column R
    D   column S

4. I was in a car race with 9 other cars. I passed five cars. Then two cars passed me. I finished in 3rd place. In which position did I start the race?

    A   4th
    B   5th
    C   6th
    D   7th

© MR STEGGELS ADVANCED INSTRUCTION PTY LTD

5. On my wall clock, the long hand is pointing to 6. The short hand is halfway between 3 and 4. What will the time be one and a half hours from now?

   A   3:30
   B   4:30
   C   5:00
   D   6:00

6. Which number is next in the series?

   101   91   82   74   67   61   ___

   A   56
   B   55
   C   54
   D   53

7. In a bag I have the following marbles: one green, two yellow, four blue, eight red, and twelve orange. How many do I have to choose before I can be certain of getting a red marble?

   A   8
   B   9
   C   19
   D   20

8. The smaller shape on the right was used to make this wall. How many smaller shapes were used?

   A   5
   B   6
   C   8
   D   10

9. Which letter must be removed from **mean** to make a word meaning **male**?

   A   m
   B   e
   C   a
   D   n

© MR STEGGELS ADVANCED INSTRUCTION PTY LTD

Read the text and answer questions 10—14

Pet Place

DOGS	CATS	BIRDS	REPTILES	FISH	SMALL ANIMALS
Earn Points As You Shop		$5.00 Delivery In City Areas		Log In To My Account	
(kitten image)				*(rabbit image)*	
			25% OFF			
			ONLINE SALES ONLY			
WE SELL				**CLICK &**	
Throw It® dog toys				**COLLECT**	
Kitty Kat Crunch®					
My Backyard® food bowls				Order online	
Best mate® collars				Pick up in store	
SALE		SPECIALS				*(fish tank image)*	
Twitchy® rabbit hutches		bird feeders					
		dog kennels					
Take an extra 10% off!		cat litter and scratching posts				Special $25 off	
		indoor pet odour spray				Clear View® fish tanks	
IDEAL HEALTH®		OPITMAX PET FOOD®		TOTAL BALANCE DIET®	

10. The terms **on sale** or **on special** mean

    A   buy it now
    B   online sales only
    C   selling at a lower price
    D $25 or 25% off

11. The author has included pictures of pets to

    A   fill up space
    B   attract the reader's attention
    C   show which animals are 25% off
    D   show the most popular pets

12. Which is true?

    A   If you order online, you have to get your items posted to you
    B   There is a special on dog walking leads
    C   If you buy from the website, you get 25% off
    D   Pet place does not sell birds

13. **Small animals** would include

    A   snakes
    B   rabbits
    C   birds
    D   none of the above

14. Which item is not on special?

    A   Twitchy® rabbit hutch
    B   Clear View® fish tank
    C   Cat scratching post
    D   Throw It® dog toy

© MR STEGGELS ADVANCED INSTRUCTION PTY LTD

15. Which shape completes the second pair in the same way as the first?

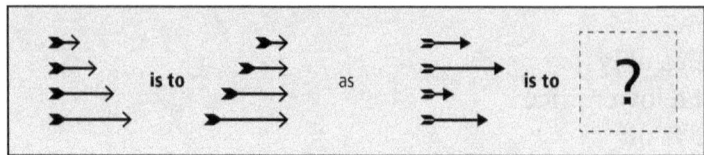

16. Thirty one chocolates were shared equally among 7 friends. How many chocolates could not be shared?

   A   1
   B   2
   C   3
   D   4

17. What would you find in a **vault**?

   A   water
   B   ships
   C   money
   D   rubbish

18. Which letters are missing in this series?

            PR   RP   ___   VL   XJ

   A   TM
   B   SO
   C   TN
   D   TO

19. Which letters must be added to **honest** to form its opposite?

   A   anti
   B   un
   C   mis
   D   dis

This bar graph is for questions 20—21

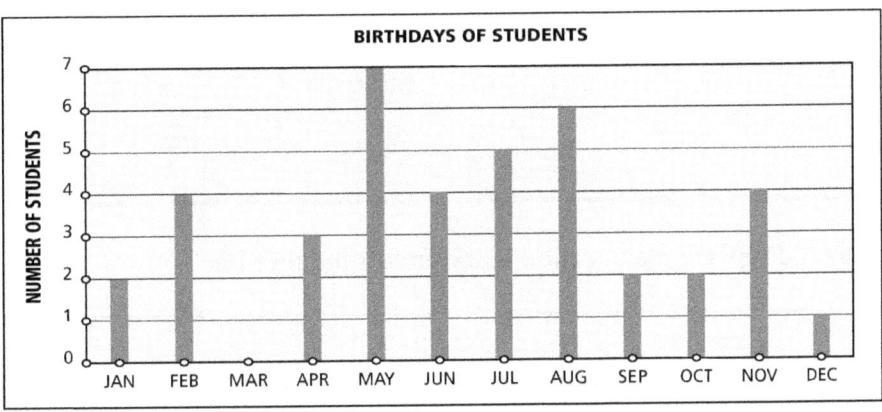

20. Which is true?

    A   There are more birthdays in June than there are in November
    B   There are more birthdays in the first three months than the last three months of the year
    C   August has the most number of birthdays
    D   January, September and October have the same number of birthdays

21. Which is false?

    A   40 students have been included in the graph
    B   There are more birthdays from May to August than September to December
    C   April and May added together make up ¼ of all birthdays
    D   December has the fewest number of birthdays

22. What is the distance around the edge of this shape?

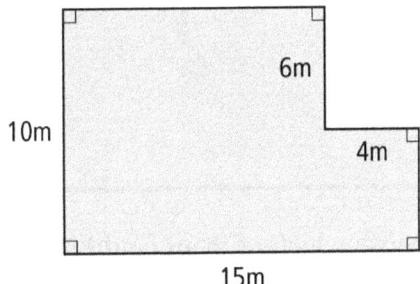

    A   25m
    B   35m
    C   50m
    D   some lengths are missing so it is impossible to calculate

© MR STEGGELS ADVANCED INSTRUCTION PTY LTD

23. Which word means **a gentle wind**?

    A   gale
    B   hurricane
    C   breeze
    D   air

24. What number should replace the question mark on this number line?

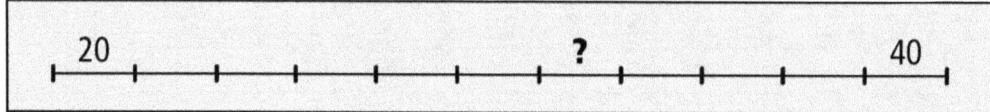

    A   30
    B   32
    C   33
    D   36

25. I am 3cm shorter than my friend Heath. Heath is 6cm taller than my friend James. James is 145cm. How tall am I?

    A   148cm
    B   147cm
    C   149cm
    D   141cm

26. If the code for **remains** is 1234567, what will the code be for **marines**?

    A   3416527
    B   3451627
    C   3415627
    D   3415623

27. Unscramble these letters and choose which of them **could not be worn**

    A   asenj
    B   uoseh
    C   itsu
    D   pace

© MR STEGGELS ADVANCED INSTRUCTION PTY LTD

28. Which tile completes the larger pattern?

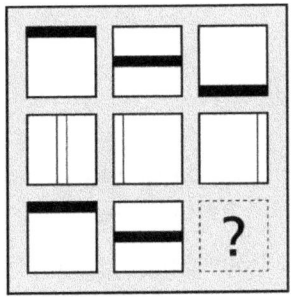
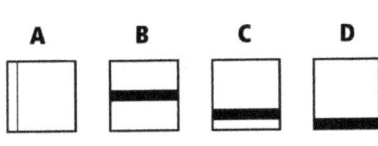

29. Which letter is next in the pattern?

A   B   D   G   ___

A   H
B   I
C   J
D   K

30. Which code should replace the question mark?

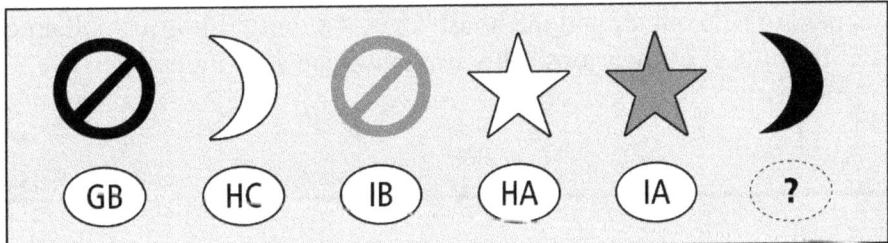

A   GC
B   HB
C   IC
D   GB

Read the text and answer questions 31—35

Should kids get paid to help out around the house?

Parents are busy. They need help around the house. Cleaning takes a lot of time. So does cooking. Many parents expect their children to help. But, should kids be paid for helping out around the house?

On one hand, kids should be paid to help out around the house. It is called pocket money. Kids should earn pocket money. Some kids get money from their parents for no reason at all. This is not right. Kids should be paid when they help out. If they do not help out, they should not get any money.

Kids like to have their own money. They will work to get it. Kids cannot work in real jobs because they are too young. But they can help around the house by sweeping the floors and carpets, doing the dishes and washing the car. This way, they can earn money. They can spend their money on things they need, like books and items for school.

On the other hand, kids should not be paid to help out around the house. Parents do not get paid for doing housework. They do not get five dollars every time they wash the dishes or take out the garbage. They just have to do it. **It** is their job. Kids should have to do it, too. For free. They should want to help their parents because they love them, not because they will get money.

Kids will not do any work at all if they expect to get paid every time. They might not even do their homework if they do not get money! Children will turn into greedy money monsters. Parents should not spoil their children in this way.

Should kids get paid to help out around the house? Yes, but only if it is a small amount, like five dollars a week. And only if they do all of their jobs. This way, kids can save money and use it to buy the things they need.

© MR STEGGELS ADVANCED INSTRUCTION PTY LTD

31. This text can best be described as

    A   an exposition—only one side of the issue is presented
    B   a discussion—both sides of the issue are presented
    C   a report about kids helping out around the house
    D   an imaginative story

32. How many paragraphs tell us why kids should be paid to help out around the house?

    A   one
    B   two
    C   three
    D   four

33. The author thinks that

    A   kids should always be paid to help out around the house
    B   kids should never be paid to help out around the house
    C   kids should be paid for helping, but only in small amounts
    D   parents should decide to pay their kids or not

34. The word **It** in paragraph 4 refers to

    A   taking out the garbage
    B   housework
    C   washing the dishes
    D   their job

35. The author thinks that if kids are paid every time they help out around the house, then they

    A   will turn into greedy money monsters
    B   might not do their homework
    C   will be spoiled
    D   all of the above

© MR STEGGELS ADVANCED INSTRUCTION PTY LTD

END OF TEST

Test 5

1. Which shape is a reflection of the shape on the left?

   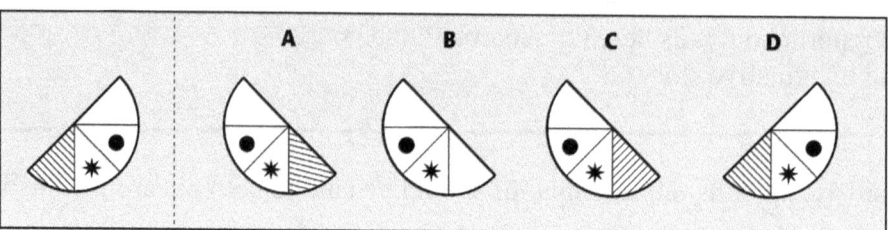

2. Which two letters can be used to end the first word and begin the second word?

   l a __ __ / __ __ o l

   A   ps
   B   co
   C   id
   D   te

This bar graph is for questions 3—4

Favourite Sandwich Fillings

| Cheese and lettuce | Honey | Egg | Ham |

3. Thirty people were asked about their favourite sandwich fillings. How many chose honey?

   A   2
   B   4
   C   6
   D   10

4. Which is true?

   A   More than half of the students in the class chose cheese and lettuce
   B   One third of the class chose egg
   C   More students chose honey than egg
   D   none of the above

© MR STEGGELS ADVANCED INSTRUCTION PTY LTD

5. I have some pet cats and pet chickens. Altogether, they have 14 legs. I have 5 pets. How many pet cats do I have?

    A   1
    B   2
    C   3
    D   4

6. The letters in **trees** can be rearranged to form a new word meaning

    A   a group of plants
    B   to turn a wheel
    C   not enough
    D   shut down

7. Which pair of words is most similar in meaning?

    A   plain   quiet
    B   enjoy   dislike
    C   agree   know
    D   injure   harm

8. **Teacher** is to **student** as _____ is to _____

    A   girl   boy
    B   dog   puppy
    C   doctor   patient
    D   petrol   car

9. When you take the smallest 2-digit number away from the largest 2-digit number, the answer is

    A   1
    B   99
    C   89
    D   88

© MR STEGGELS ADVANCED INSTRUCTION PTY LTD

10. To **prepare** means to

    A   start something
    B   set the table for dinner
    C   invent something new
    D   get ready

11. In my class there are 25 students. 16 students play soccer. 14 students play tennis. Some do both. 5 students do not play soccer or tennis. How many students play both soccer and tennis?

    A   2
    B   5
    C   10
    D   25

12. If the code for **hardest** is 7654321, what will the code be for **threads**?

    A   1723625
    B   1754632
    C   1753642
    D   none of the above

13. It takes me 10 minutes to walk to school. It takes me the same time to walk back home. How many minutes do I spend walking to school and back in one school week?

    A   20 minutes
    B   60 minutes
    C   100 minutes
    D   140 minutes

14. These words all have something in common. Which word also belongs in this group?

    gum   ankle   shoulder   tongue

    A   palm
    B   tree
    C   walk
    D   boy

© MR STEGGELS ADVANCED INSTRUCTION PTY LTD

15. Which pair of words is most opposite in meaning?

    A   let   allow
    B   think   watch
    C   create destroy
    D   quit   stop

16. Which is next in the series?

    @   @@   @@@   @@@@
    $$$$$ $$$$ $$$ $$?
    %   %   %   %

    @@@@@   @@@@   @@@@@   @@@@@
               $ $ $$
    %   %%%   %   %
    A   B   C   D

17. Here are the first 3 shapes in a pattern. How many grey squares will be needed to make the 5th shape?

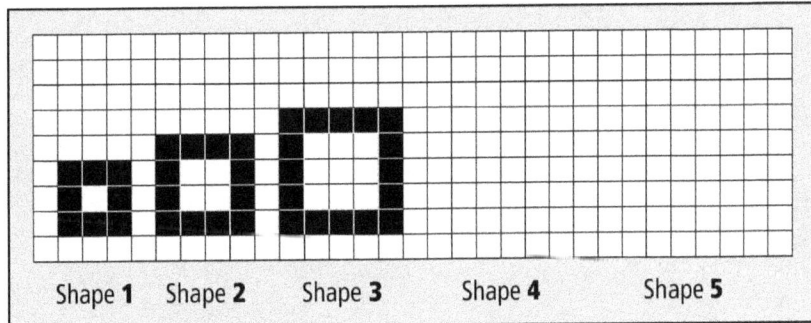

Shape 1   Shape 2   Shape 3   Shape 4   Shape 5

    A   24
    B   25
    C   36
    D   40

18. Which phrase means **something that is very easy to do**?

    A   a toss up
    B   a drop in the bucket
    C   a bird in the hand is worth two in the bush
    D   a piece of cake

© MR STEGGELS ADVANCED INSTRUCTION PTY LTD

Read the text and answer questions 19—23

My new bike

See my new bike?
It shines in the sun
I got it for Christmas
From Grandad and Mum

See my new bike?
It's silver and black
There's not a scratch on it
I hope I don't stack!

See my new bike?
It has the best tyres
With a look and a feel
Everybody admires

See my new bike?
The chain is on tight
The frame is well-built
The seat is just right

I'm ready to race
My feet on the pedals
Ready, set, go!
I want to win medals

My new bike is fast
Make no mistakes
It goes like a rocket
Now…where are the brakes?

© MR STEGGELS ADVANCED INSTRUCTION PTY LTD

19. This text is a

    A   narrative
    B   recount
    C   diary entry
    D   poem

20. What does **stack** mean?

    A   go too fast
    B   track
    C   crash
    D   drop it

21. Why does the poet keep repeating **See my new bike?**

    A   It rhymes
    B   The poet really wants people to notice the new bike
    C   Poems always have lines that are repeated
    D   No one is really interested in the new bike

22. What is it about the new bike that everybody admires?

    A   It is shiny and new
    B   The tyres look and feel great
    C   It is very well built
    D   It goes like rocket

23. The last line in the poem is meant to

    A   make the reader laugh
    B   frighten the reader
    C   warn the reader to always check the brakes on a new bike
    D   make the poet crash

© MR STEGGELS ADVANCED INSTRUCTION PTY LTD

24. Which figure completes the pattern?

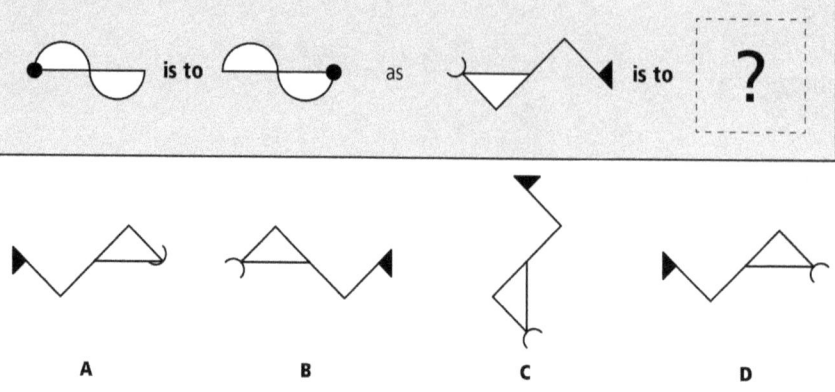

This chart is for questions 25—26

Student	Test 1	Test 2	Test 3	Test 4
Alison	10	9	6	8
Bill	8	5	10	8
Celine	6	10	7	9
Dillum	9	6	10	7

25. Which students scored the same total for the four tests?

    A   Alison and Bill
    B   Celine and Bill
    C   Alison and Dillum
    D   Celine and Dillum

26. Which is true?

    A   All students scored above 30
    B   Alison had the highest total score
    C   Bill had the lowest total score
    D   all of the above

27. A **group of wolves** is called a

    A   team
    B   fight
    C   gang
    D   pack

© MR STEGGELS ADVANCED INSTRUCTION PTY LTD

28. Lorna is 8 years older than Gina. Frank is twice as old as Colin. Gina is one year younger than Colin. Colin is 6 years old. How many years separate Frank and Lorna?

    A   1 year
    B   2 years
    C   3 years
    D   4 years

29. Which code should replace the question mark?

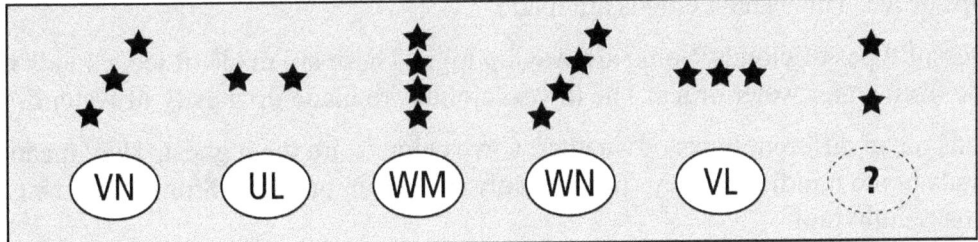

    A   UN
    B   UM
    C   WL
    D   VM

30. Which letter can be added to end of these letters?

    hai__ coa__ coi__ leve__

    A   r
    B   l
    C   t
    D   z

© MR STEGGELS ADVANCED INSTRUCTION PTY LTD

Read the text and answer questions 31—35

What are clouds?

Clouds float in the sky. Sometimes they are white and fluffy. Sometimes they are grey and cover the sky like a blanket. They make the daytime dark.

Clouds are made of tiny drops of water. The drops can also be frozen as ice crystals.

The air around us has water in it. When warm air goes up high in the sky, it gets cooler. The water in the air turns into drops or ice. This is how clouds are made.

There are different types of clouds. Some are way up high. These are made of ice. Clouds in the middle layer can be made from either water or ice. The lowest clouds are made up mostly of water drops.

Different clouds mean different types of weather. Cirrus clouds are the highest. They mean good weather. The clouds in the middle are grey. They usually bring rain or snow. Stratus are low clouds. They are flat and can make light rain.

Some clouds are very tall—they start low and stretch all the way to up into the sky. They cause thunderstorms, hail and even tornadoes. They are called cumulonimbus clouds.

Clouds are very heavy. They can stay up in the air because warm air from below keeps pushing them up.

There are ten main cloud types:

- High clouds—cirrus, cirrocumulus, cirrostratus
- Middle clouds—altostratus, altocumulus, nimbostratus
- Low cloud—stratus, stratocumulus
- Vertical—cumulus, cumulonimbus

Did you know?

Clouds can travel very fast—up to one hundred and sixty kilometers in one hour!

© MR STEGGELS ADVANCED INSTRUCTION PTY LTD

31. The main purpose of this text is to

   A   entertain the reader with a story about clouds
   B   explain how clouds are made
   C   get the reader to agree that clouds are very interesting
   D   retell a series of events about clouds

32. Clouds are formed

   A   because of different types of weather
   B   to make rain
   C   as warm air keeps pushing them up
   D   when warm air cools down

33. The clouds that usually bring rain or snow are

   A   the highest
   B   in the middle layer
   C   lowest to the ground
   D   very tall and heavy

34. We can conclude that the highest clouds

   A   are colder than the clouds beneath them
   B   are warmer than the clouds beneath them
   C   are the same temperature as the clouds beneath them
   D   cause the worst weather

35. Which is not a type of cloud?

   A   cirrocumulus
   B   nimbostratus
   C   cirrus
   D   stratonimbus

© MR STEGGELS ADVANCED INSTRUCTION PTY LTD

END OF TEST

Test 1 solutions

Q	A	Explanation
1	A	These are the stages of a baby's growth. It describes the changes that a baby goes through at each age.
2	A	This text gives information about what skills a baby develops and at which time.
3	C	Birth to 3 months—make a fist
4	B	1 to 2 years—turn knobs and handles
5	D	9 to 12 months—pick up and throw objects
6	D	skip one letter: G H I J K L M N O
7	D	The total distance around the edge is called the perimeter. It is made up of two lengths and two widths → 11 + 11 + 6 + 6 = 34 metres
8	D	and = 5V% got = K7& d = % o = 7 n = v g = k
9	C	12 + 7 = 19 19 – 3 = 16
10	D	Rude means bad mannered. Polite means well-mannered. There is no such word as unrude. The opposite to happy is sad. The opposite to okay is unwell, unsatisfactory, unacceptable.
11	B	The circle is inside and the square is outside. In A, C and D, the square is inside and the circle is outside.
12	B	swamp does not sound the same as stamp, damp and clamp rhyme.
13	A	Add (2 + 10 = 12) Difference (10 – 2 = 8)
14	D	2 x 6 = 12 then 12 – 5 = 7
15	C	outline outside outrun outfit
16	B	Like two peas in a pod means so similar that it is hard to tell them apart. Peas look identical to each other.
17	C	A, B and D are all opinions. It is a fact that the best friends watch the same television shows and listen to the same music.
18	D	A birthday party is arranged, not sorted or shaped. Celebrate does not mean the same as organise.
19	D	Sarah is two months older than the author. The author's birthday is in July. Sarah must have been born two months earlier in May.
20	A	Our mothers became friends right away, so we started playing together.
21	B	A: a vegetarian does not eat meat B: a greengrocer sells fruits and vegetables. C: a landlord manages/owns a building that people rent D: a green keeper looks after the grass on a golf course
22	B	Top number in table – 3 then x 2 9 – 3 = 6 6 x 2 = 12 ; 10 – 3 = 7 7 x 2 = 14 ; 8 – 3 = 5 5 x 2 = 10 ; 5 – 3 = 2 2 x 2 = 4
23	C	The possible numbers are: 1, 2, 3, 4, 5 & 6. Three of these numbers are even (2, 4 & 6). There is a 3 out of 6 chance of rolling an even number. 3 out of 6 is the same as 1 out of 2
24	C	parsley, mint and basil are herbs. A clam is seafood in a shell.
25	C	6 small squares + 2 (2 x 2) squares left and right
26	A	easy is the opposite of difficult. Fresh is the opposite of rotten.

27	A	John: 2.01m – 1.85m = 16cm Sarah: 1.66m – 1.56m = 10cm Ali: 2.13m – 2.02m = 11cm Chivani 2.25m – 2.10m = 15cm
28	D	The teacher told his students to sit still.
29	C	h = 3, e = 9, a = 8, t = 5, teeth = 59953
30	C	Nine of the children chose netball. This is one quarter of the sector graph. 9 children chose cricket. 18 children chose soccer. 9 + 9 + 18 = 36
31	C	A = thumb B = foot C = walk D = heart
32	B	The sequence is repeated after five shapes. The diamond divided into four diamonds follows the diamond with the vertical line in the centre
33	B	Before I had $3 left over, I spent $2. So I had $5 after I gave my friend half my money. I had $10 to begin with. $10 ÷ 2 = $5 $5 - $2 = $3
34	A	1st pair: triangles become semi-circles. The centre rectangle does not change shape or size.
35	C	Each letter matches an even number in order | A	B	C	D	E	F	G	H	I	J	K	L	M	N
---	---	---	---	---	---	---	---	---	---	---	---	---	---
2	4	6	8	10	12	14	16	18	20	22	24	26	28	

Test 1 score summary

General ability	Question	6	8	10	11	12	15	21	24	26	28	29	31	32	34	35	Total
	tick/cross																
Reading	Question	1	2	3	4	5	16	17	18	19	20	Total					
	tick/cross																
Mathematics	Question	7	9	13	14	22	23	25	27	30	33	Total					
	tick/cross																

Test 2 solutions

Q	A	Explanation
1	C	Thomas has been transported to another time. The animals he hears are probably no longer alive today.
2	C	Thomas thought the watch was a piece of junk (paragraph 4) The watch started to glow and hum (paragraph 4) The watch got warm (paragraph 9) A huge head appeared from the bushes (paragraph 12)
3	B	wound is the past tense of wind (sounds like mind) wound sounds like ground.
4	C	After Thomas winds the watch by turning the knob on the side, the hands start to spin and he is taken to another place and time.
5	B	Buildings as high as the clouds, flying cars and people floating around on boards—none of these things are possible yet. Thomas is in the future.
6	D	To turn your back on someone is to ignore them—to give them none of your attention.
7	A	Finish and end are similar in meaning. Crooked and bent are similar in meaning.
8	C	Mules are known for not doing what they are ordered if they think it might place them in danger. A mule is a cross between a female horse and a male donkey.
9	B	The numbers are 8 and 4. 4 x 2 = 8 8 + 4 = 12 8 – 4 = 4
10	C	This pattern needs to be 5 x 5 squares = 25. There are 15 squares. 10 more are needed.

11	D	Math problems and math games start at 11:30am and finish at 1:00pm. That is 90 minutes.
12	A	Lunch is 60 minutes. Recess is 20 minutes.
13	D	The doctor said to get some rest.
14	C	The box is 3cm wide, 3cm high and 3cm long. It can fit 3 sugar cubes along its width, 3 sugar cubes along its length and 3 sugar cubes stack up; 3 x 3 x 3 = 27
15	D	Passengers board an aeroplane.
16	B	8 x 3 = 24 4 x 6 = 24
17	A	Milk is stored/put into a carton. Flowers are stored/put into a vase.
18	C	There are 6 x 4 squares = 24. Each square is worth ½ . ½ of 24 = 12
19	D	From school to the sign is 5km. From the sign to the shop is 6km. 5km + 6km = 11km.
20	B	A: has a black rectangle B: is the mirror image / reflection of the shape on the left C: There is no line to show the semi-circle D: The shape has been translated
21	B	Take the last two letters of the 1st word and the last two letters of the 2nd word. deli +soft = lift
22	C	pickup: to collect something or someone. Another name for a truck upload: to send or save a file to a server on the Internet
23	D	alert → later which means at a time in the future
24	A	1 + 2 + 3 + 4 + 5 + 6 + 7 + 8 = 36 Sam made 8 stops in delivering 36 flowers
25	D	The small black star is moving anti-clockwise as the pattern moves from left to right
26	B	If something grows it gets bigger or increases.
27	A	These are all types of weather. A thunderstorm is a type of weather
28	D	The letters is stare can be used to form rates, taser and tears
29	D	All even numbers between 40 and 52: 42, 44, 46, 48, 50 → five in total
30	C	A kitchen is a place where food is prepared and cooked, so there must be an oven.
31	B	This text is meant for kids who want to make their own hat. The author writes your Easter hat parade and Have a great time at your Easter hat parade in your colourful hat.
32	C	Step 4: Glue or staple cardboard strip into a circle with overlap.
33	C	Step 6: Carefully cut out the stencils Step 8: Decorate the hat with glitter glue Step 5: Colour in Easter stencils with crayons Step 3: Cut a strip of cardboard
34	C	Steps 7 and 8 can be swapped. Both are glue decorations and can be done in either order.
35	B	Step 6: Carefully (is an adverb—it tells you HOW to cut the stencils)

Test 2 score summary

General ability	Question	6	7	8	13	15	17	20	21	22	23	25	26	27	28	30	Total
	tick/cross																
Reading	Question	1	2	3	4	5	31	32	33	34	35	Total					
	tick/cross																
Mathematics	Question	9	10	11	12	14	16	18	19	24	29	Total					
	tick/cross																

Test 3 solutions

Q	A	Explanation
1	D	Both the Queen and the Jack are to the left of the King. The King is on the far right. The Queen is to the left of the Jack. The Jack is in the middle.
2	C	A group of people is called a crowd. A group of sheep is called a flock.
3	B	tied (1) attached with string tide (2) rising and falling of the sea
4	B	p = % o = # s = @ h = ! h = ! o = # p = % s = @
5	D	$5.00 - $1.65 = $3.35
6	A	If a surface is smooth, it is flat or even.
7	D	There are six square faces in a cube.
8	B	The pattern is + 1 then + 2 then + 3 then + 4 then + 5 16 + 6 = 22
9	C	A house always has walls. Without them, the house cannot stand.
10	C	Playing in the water can be lots of fun. But it can also be dangerous. The word but tells us that the opposite meaning is coming in the sentence. Fun is opposite to dangerous.
11	D	Make sure that everyone knows how to swim. If not, they need (swimming) lessons.
12	A	Some rocks have shells on them that are very sharp. Spiders, logs and glass can also hurt you.
13	C	Always swim between the flags at the beach. The lifesavers set up the flags at the safest part of the beach. They also watch this section closely.
14	D	Very cold water can make it hard for you to breathe.
15	B	Shape A has 4 triangles. Shape B is made up of 24 triangles. 4 x 6 = 24. If you rotate shape B so that the side is at the top, rather than the corner, then you can see the pattern more easily.
16	C	triangular prism (6 corners) rectangular prism (8 corners) square pyramid (5 corners) cube (8 corners)
17	A	The white octagon becomes smaller & the black octagon becomes larger The white triangle must become smaller & the black star must become larger
18	D	A trifle is a dessert made from sponge cake, jelly, custard and cream.
19	D	Group A: hand Group B: shake = handshake
20	C	he = 45 oh = 74 so = 67 h = 4 e = 5 o = 7 s = 6 shoe = 6475

21	D	dash: to run in a hurry hint: a small piece of information or advice, a clue
22	C	4 out of 8 squares are shaded. This is ½ .
23	C	The time on the clock is 8.30am. Recess is at 10.00am. That is one hour (60 minutes) and 30 minutes later. 60 minutes + 30 minutes = 90 minutes
24	A	Pattern: jump 1 letter backwards Q R H I L M V W Z A W X
25	C	tabu → tuba
26	B	To do something at the drop of a hat means to do it right away, or ready to do it right away.
27	C	chance of spinning white = 2 out of 8 chance of spinning black = 1 out of 8 chance of spinning yellow= 3 out of 8 chance of spinning green = 2 out of 8 The spinner will land on yellow 3 out of every 8 times. This might not happen on the first 8 spins, but it will happen the more you spin.
28	B	If Friday was one day ago, it is now Saturday. One week from Saturday is Saturday.
29	D	Each shape should have three small black stars and two small black circles.
30	C	I swam across the lake to the island.
31	B	This is a recount text about Howie's day at the zoo. There are many words that show the passing of time (After lunch, next, on the way back to school, first), and the events are in order.
32	B	James took Howie's class to see the dolphin and sea lion show (paragraph 9). Lunch time happens between paragraphs 9 and 10
33	A	A zookeeper came with a basket of bananas (paragraph 8) Howie saw the giraffes being fed (paragraph 7) The sea lion clapped his flippers (paragraph 9) Howie's teacher told him to wait at the entrance (paragraph 4)
34	D	Lions are kept separate from other animals because they are predators that hunt and kill. Giraffes, elephants and zebras are not meat eaters.
35	C	Howie sat patiently while the other kids turned up. He was first to arrive at the classroom.

Test 3 score summary																
General ability	Question	2	3	4	6	9	17	18	19	20	21	24	25	26	29	30	Total
	tick/cross																
Reading	Question	10	11	12	13	14	31	32	33	34	35	Total				
	tick/cross															
Mathematics	Question	1	5	7	8	15	16	22	23	27	28	Total				
	tick/cross															

Test 4 solutions

Q	A	Explanation
1	B	meats → steam which is a white mist of water
2	B	Pizza is very popular at a birthday party.
3	A	<table><tr><th>P</th><th>Q</th><th>R</th><th>S</th></tr><tr><td>1</td><td>2</td><td>3</td><td>4</td></tr><tr><td>8</td><td>7</td><td>6</td><td>5</td></tr><tr><td>9</td><td>10</td><td>11</td><td>12</td></tr><tr><td>16</td><td>15</td><td>14</td><td>13</td></tr><tr><td>17</td><td>18</td><td>19</td><td>20</td></tr><tr><td>24</td><td>23</td><td>22</td><td>21</td></tr></table>
4	C	Start of race: 1, 2, 3, 4, 5, Me, 7, 8, 9, 10 (I began in 6th position) During race: Me, 2, 3, 4, 5, 6, 7, 8, 9. 10 (I passed five cars to get to 1st place) End of race: 1, 2, Me, 4, 5, 6, 7, 8, 9, 10 (Two cars passed me and I ended up in 3rd)
5	C	The time now is 3:30. One and a half hours later is 5:00
6	A	The pattern is – 10, – 9, – 8, – 7, – 6, – 5. 61 – 5 = 56
7	C	The only way to be certain of picking a red marble from the bag is if there are only red marbles in the bag. So, every other colour must be removed first. 1 green, 2 yellow, 4 blue and 12 orange = 19. On my 20th pick, there will only be red marbles left.
8	B	There are 18 squares in the wall. The smaller shape is 3 squares. 18 ÷ 3 = 6
9	B	mean take away e → man. A man is a male.
10	C	On sale and on special mean that the original price has been lowered. This can be a certain amount or by a percentage taken off the price. (e.g. 10% off $100 is $10, so the new price would be $90)
11	B	The pictures of pets are meant to attract the attention of the reader.
12	C	25% off online sales only—if you buy online (from the website) you get 25% off. The answer is not A you can buy online and pick up in store → Click and collect
13	B	A snakes are found in the reptiles section B rabbits are found in the small animals section C birds already have their own section
14	D	Throw It® dog toys are sold at Pet Place, they are not on special.
15	B	All lines are aligned to the right hand side (they all end on the right). A is incorrect because the lines have be rearranged in order from smallest at the top to longest at the bottom. The arrows in C are facing the wrong way. The vanes in D are all black.
16	C	31 divided by 4 → 7 x 4 = 28 31 – 28 = 3
17	C	A vault is where valuables such as money and jewels are kept safe.
18	C	1st letter: P q R s T u V w X (skip one forward) 2nd letter: R q P o N m L k J (skip one backward)

19	D	The opposite of honest is dishonest.
20	D	There are 2 birthdays in January, September and October
21	D	March has the fewest number of birthdays → zero
22	C	The length missing at the top of the shape is 15m – 4m = 11m. The length missing on the right on the shape is 10m – 6m = 4m Adding these lengths together: 15m + 10m + 11m + 6m + 4m + 4m = 50m
23	C	A breeze is a gentle wind. A gale and a hurricane are very strong winds. Air is the invisible gas surrounding the earth.
24	B	Each rectangle on the number line is a jump of 2 → 20, 22, 24, 26, 28, 30, 32, 34, 36, 38, 50
25	A	James is 145cm. Heath is 6 cm taller. 145cm + 6cm = 151cm I am 3 cm shorter than Heath. 151cm – 3cm = 148cm
26	C	m = 3 a = 4 r = 1 i = 5 n = 6 e = 2 s = 7 → 3415627
27	B	A = jeans B = house C = suit D = cape
28	D	The top row is repeated in the bottom row.
29	D	Pattern: skip 0, skip 1, skip 2, skip 3 → A B c D e f G h i j K
30	A	G = black A = star H = white B = circle with diagonal line I = checkered C = crescent moon
31	B	This text is a discussion argument. Both sides of the issue are presented: Kids should / should not get paid.
32	B	Paragraphs 2 and 3 tell us why kids should be paid to help out around the house.
33	C	Paragraph 6: Should kids get paid to help out around the house? Yes, but only if it is a small amount, like five dollars a week.
34	B	Parents do not get paid for doing housework. They do not get five dollars every time they wash the dishes or take out the garbage. They just have to do it. It is their job. And kids should have to do it, too.
35	D	Kids will not do any work at all if they expect to get paid every time. They might not even do their homework if they do not get money! Children will turn into greedy money monsters. Parents should not spoil their children in this way.

Test 4 score summary																
General ability	Question	1	2	3	6	9	15	17	18	19	23	26	27	28	29	30	Total
	tick/cross																
Reading	Question	10	11	12	13	14	31	32	33	34	35	Total					
	tick/cross																
Mathematics	Question	4	5	7	8	16	20	21	22	24	25	Total					
	tick/cross																

Test 5 solutions

Q	A	Explanation
1	C	A: the diagonal lines are in the wrong direction B: There is no pattern in the bottom segment D: the shape has been translated
2	C	id can be added to both → laid and idol laid = past tense of lay idol = someone who is admired very much
3	C	Each segment or rectangle of the bar graph = 3 people. 30 ÷ 10 = 3 Honey = 2 segments = 2 x 3 = 6
4	D	A: 12 out of 30 people chose cheese and lettuce. This is not more than half. B: 9 out of 30 chose egg. This is not one third.
5	B	cats have 4 legs chickens have 2 legs. 2 cats = 8 legs. 3 chickens = 6 legs 6 + 8 = 14 legs altogether 2 cats + 3 chickens = 5 pets altogether
6	B	trees becomes steer which means to turn a wheel and control the movement of a vehicle
7	D	injure and harm have similar meanings
8	C	A teacher takes care of a student. A doctor takes care of a patient.
9	C	The smallest 2-digit number is 10. The largest 2-digit number is 99. 99 – 10 = 89
10	D	prepare means to get something ready to use or get ready to do something
11	C	In the class of 25, 5 students do not play soccer or tennis. That leaves 20 students who play soccer, tennis or both. Altogether, 30 students play soccer, tennis or both, So, 10 students must play both.
12	C	t = 1 h = 7 r = 5 e = 3 a = 6 d = 4 s = 2
13	C	Each day I walk for 20 minutes (to school and back). There are five days in a school week. 20 x 5 = 100 minutes.
14	A	These are all body parts. The palm is the inside surface of your hand.
15	C	destroy is the opposite of create.
16	C	top line: @ increases by one to 5 middle line: $ decreases by one to 1 bottom line: % remains the same (1)
17	A	1st shape = 8 squares, 2nd shape = 12 squares, 3rd shape = 16 squares, 4th shape = 20 squares, 5th shape = 24 squares
18	D	a toss up: A result that is still unclear and can go either way. a drop in the bucket: A very small part of something big or whole. a bird in the hand is worth two in the bush: Having something that is certain is much better than taking a risk for more, because chances are you might lose everything. a piece of cake: Very easy to achieve
19	D	This is a poem. There are verses. The 2nd and 4th lines rhyme.
20	C	To stack means to crash

21	B	The poet wants everyone to notice and like the new bike.
22	B	See my new bike? It has the best tyres With a look and a feel Everybody admires
23	A	The last line is meant to make the reader laugh. The poet has listed all the great things about the bike but has totally forgotten to check for the brakes!
24	D	The first shape has been rotated a ½ turn. When the second shape is rotated a 1/2 turn, the triangle must turn upside down, the black triangle must be on the left and the semi circle must face south east instead of north west
25	D	Alison: 33 Bill: 31 Celine: 32 Dillum: 32
26	D	All students scored above 30. Alison had the highest total score. Bill had the lowest score.
27	D	A group of wolves is called a pack
28	A	Colin is 6. Gina is 5 (one year younger). Frank is 12 (twice as old as Colin) Lorna is 8 years older than Gina (8 + 5 = 13) Lorna is 13. Frank is 12. There is 1 year between them.
29	B	U = 2 dots L = horizontal V = 3 dots M = vertical W = 4 dots N = diagonal
30	B	hail coal coil level
31	B	This text answers the question 'What are clouds?' It explains what clouds are and how they are made.
32	D	Clouds are made when warm air goes up high in the sky and it gets cooler. The water turns into drops or ice. (paragraph 3)
33	B	The clouds in the middle are grey. They usually bring rain or snow. (paragraph 6)
34	A	The highest clouds are made from ice crystals. This means that they must be colder than the clouds below them which are made from water drops and ice. (paragraph 4)
35	D	Stratonimbus is not listed under the section There are ten main cloud types.

Test 5 score summary																
General ability	Question	1	2	6	7	8	10	12	14	15	16	18	24	27	29	30	Total
	tick/cross																
Reading	Question	19	20	21	22	23	31	32	33	34	35	Total				
	tick/cross															
Mathematics	Question	3	4	5	9	11	13	17	25	26	28	Total				
	tick/cross															

www.ingramcontent.com/pod-product-compliance
Lightning Source LLC
LaVergne TN
LVHW061316060426
835507LV00019B/2185